Editor
Polly Hoffman

Editorial Project Manager
Mara Ellen Guckian

Editor-in-Chief
Sharon Coan, M.S. Ed.

Illustrators
Kevin Barnes
Renée Christine Yates

Cover Artist
Barb Lorseyedi

Art Coordinator
Kevin Barnes

Art Director
Cjae Froshay

Imaging
Ralph Olmedo, Jr.
James Edward Grace

Product Manager
Phil Garcia

Publisher
Mary D. Smith, M.S. Ed.

Full Color

Literacy Centers for Reading Skills

Pre K–1

Authors

Dede Dodds, M.S. Ed. & Traci Clausen, M.S. Ed.

Teacher Created Resources

Teacher Created Resources, Inc.
6421 Industry Way
Westminster, CA 92683
www.teachercreated.com
ISBN-0-7439-3702-3
©2003 Teacher Created Resources, Inc.
Reprinted, 2005
Made in U.S.A.

Table of Contents

Introduction

Purposeful practice is essential for improvement and mastery of literacy skills. All students can experience literacy success, given proper instruction, materials, and plenty of opportunities to practice. Primary teachers will find *Literacy Centers for Reading Skills (Pre K–1)* invaluable in providing this much-needed practice. The centers should be used to review and reinforce the language skills and objectives taught as part of your reading, writing, listening, and speaking curriculum.

This book includes meaningful, easy-to-create, easy-to-manage, independent activities for primary classrooms. These literacy centers supply the independent practice that is a natural follow-up to whole class instruction. Teacher-directed lessons are most effective if the materials and activities involved are available to small groups or individuals for further investigation. Students need to practice what they have learned in order to assimilate the new information into their current knowledge base. Through centers, students gain opportunities to manipulate, repeat, share, and expand upon the presented materials at their own pace.

Grade-level and/or ability-level adjustments should be made as teachers create the literacy centers. Center directions inform teachers of all the necessary materials and preparation. Centers should be created to accomodate standards and to incorporate current classroom texts, sight word lists, etc.

Keep in mind that children learn best when they are actively involved in their own learning process. Classrooms incorporating literacy centers into their daily routine become less teacher-directed and more student-driven. As students work the centers, they learn to think critically, make decisions, and solve problems. They also demonstrate the personal characteristics of responsibility, self-esteem, self-management, and integrity needed to function in society.

What You Will Find in This Book

There are several literacy center activities for each section. Each literacy center begins with an objective. The teacher's instructions are presented in several steps. These instructions allow the teacher to present the activity as a directed, whole-group activity prior to placing it in a center. The italicized text can serve as a script for teachers when presenting the lessons.

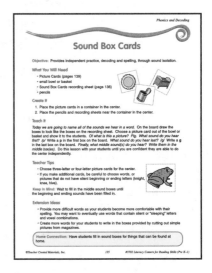

Each teacher page includes details about what you will need, how to create the manipulatives for the center, how to present the center, tips for teaching it, things to keep in mind, extension ideas, and home connection suggestions.

There is a student task card for each literacy center with simple instructions designed to remind the student what to do during the activity. Reading sheets and patterns are included when appropriate.

What Is a Literacy Center?

A literacy center is an effective teaching tool developed to support whole-group instruction. Literacy centers offer teachers a way to engage students of various abilities in active learning. Literacy centers allow students to work independently, thus freeing up the teacher to focus on differentiated instruction. Centers are designed to provide inviting activities where one or more students can work independently at a given time. Various learning tasks, along with various degrees of teacher interaction, are involved.

Centers provide learning motivation by making practice fun and non-threatening. The literacy centers in this book are process-oriented. The centers offer opportunities for students to practice new skills and to problem solve at their own pace.

Students need time to practice what they have learned once the standards, skills, and objectives have been presented by the teacher. Students need time to practice and to interact with the materials in order to set the skills (objectives) and master them.

Why Are Literacy Centers Valuable?

An optimal learning environment is created when whole-group, teacher-directed, instructional periods are combined with reinforcement and independent practice in student literacy centers. Too often in the educational process, the emphasis is placed on teaching, rather than on learning. A literacy center places the emphasis on the individual needs of each student. Research affirms the value of literacy centers and emphasizes several instructional advantages:

- Literacy centers address different learning styles better than paper and pencil tasks; they also motivate students more by providing varied stimulating activities. (Wait & Stephens, 1989)

- Literacy centers result in improved communication between home and school. (Optiz, 1995)

- Literacy centers play an important role in meeting the needs of each child. (Huyett, 1994)

Literacy centers managed in small groups create cooperative learning relationships. Learning language is a social activity. In most situations, centers allow classmates (no matter what the level) opportunities to bounce ideas off each other and to practice new skills.

There is no better way for students to truly learn a skill or concept than to work together to communicate among classmates and teach others what they have mastered.

The Language Arts Components

There are three language arts components included in *Literacy Centers for Reading Skills, (Pre K–1)*:

- Sight Words
- Phonics and Decoding
- Reading and Writing Responses

Sight Words

The Sight Words component deals with the first hundred most commonly used sight words (per Dr. Fry). These sight words have been scientifically determined to be the most commonly used words in the English language. This list is a basic tool for reading and writing teachers, curriculum developers, literacy tutors, authors of children's books, and researchers.

Sight words are words that appear over and over again in written text. These words must be internalized, or memorized, so that each of these "high frequency" words can be read by sight and do not need to be sounded out. The ability to read these words instantly greatly increases reading fluency and comprehension. The activities found in the Sight Words component will expedite retention of these important words.

Another reason for learning sight words is that many of these frequently used words do not follow regular phonics rules. For example, how do you sound out *of* or *said*? The answer is that beginning readers need to learn to read these words by "sight." Beginning writers also need to learn to spell these common words.

Phonics and Decoding

Phonics and decoding skills are practiced in any lesson or activity that includes print. Whenever a student is hearing sounds while attending to print, phonics instruction and practice are occurring. Phonics and decoding refers to the association of letters (graphemes) and the sounds (phonemes) they represent. The application of these phonics skills to read and to write is refered to as "decoding and encoding."

A key strategy in this component is to group words with similar patterns or rimes (phonograms). In word families like *cat, sat, flat*, or *king, ring, wing*, each word contains the same pattern or "chunk." In *The Reading Teacher* (1998, p. 61) Edward Fry identified 38 rimes that make up 654 different one-syllable words. Once the pattern is internalized, readers can generalize to other words with similar rhymes. This component includes most frequently used chunks or rimes as identified by researchers (Wylie & Durrell, 1970; Fry, 1998).

Reading and Writing Responses

Responding to different forms of literature enables students to voice their own opinions, demonstrate their comprehension of the text, and share their interpretations of the story. A natural way for students to explore the phonics of language is to respond in writing to what they have heard or read. Frequent writing will do more to increase spelling achievement than any other single activity. Writing helps the student discover the function of alphabetic spelling and the way words are formed.

What is the Teacher's Role

Teachers implementing *Literacy Centers for Reading Skills (Pre K–1)* in their classrooms should do the following as part of their preparation and presentation of a center:

- Choose appropriate center activities for the ability and developmental levels of students.

- Select literacy centers based on specific curriculum standards.

- Teach skills, objectives, and concepts formally through whole-group lessons prior to implementing independent activities.

- Create and set up fun, attractive, and motivating centers.

- Establish a classroom management plan clearly defining expectations.

- Explain procedures and demonstrate particular behaviors for each center.

- Afford opportunities to interact with and practice previously taught skills at the centers.

- Create a non-threatening, supportive learning environment for all students.

- Monitor student progress toward mastery by assessing student performances and/or student recording sheets.

- Give meaningful feedback, re-teaching and adjusting when necessary.

- Offer extensions and challenges when appropriate.

Standards and Assessments

In this section you will find a grid detailing the literacy standards practiced using the activities suggested. *Literacy Centers for Reading Skills (Pre K–1)* was designed with the Pre K–1 teacher in mind. Therefore, the standards met by the book go across these grade levels and fit well within broad literacy standards.

Teachers will find information within this section on both formal and informal assessment with respect to the use of literacy centers. The main objective for centers is to facilitate small-group teaching and practice among students.

Formal assessment is not an emphasis of this book. Due to the nature of centers, student assessment is not always concrete or authentic. However, there are different ways to assess student progress toward mastery. Students demonstrate their development of concept knowledge in a variety of ways. Listed below are assessment alternatives that keep the students accountable for their learning.

✿ Recording Answers

Provide students with recording sheets. Instructions for each recording sheet will vary based on the activities and concepts being practiced. The sheets should be collected and reviewed. A response, although not always necessary, can be given in the form of a sticker, a note, or a grade.

✿ Checking Each Other

When working cooperatively, young learners naturally monitor each other and provide support. Encourage them to work with and check each other. If a student feels that another student may have the wrong answer, the student performing the activity may try again. In doing this, all of the students are engaged and encouraged.

✿ Getting an "Expert"

Identify a child who has mastered the center. Assign him or her the job of being that center's "expert." Instruct students to ask the "expert" to come to the center (even if it is necessary to interrupt him or her) and check their work. Often the mini-lesson given by that classmate is a more effective one than that of the paid expert (the classroom teacher). Teach the "expert" to "instruct" with words, not his or her hands.

✿ Using an Answer Key

Answer keys for center activities can be placed in various places for student use. Below are some options for Answer Key usage:

- Set aside a place in the classroom (teacher's desk, counter, extra desk, etc.) where answer keys can be found.
- Provide an answer key with the center materials.
- Assign a student the position of "answer key monitor." That student will pass out answer keys to those students who have completed the assigned task.

Standards and Benchmarks

1 **Demonstrates competence in the general skills and strategies of the writing process**

1a *Uses prewriting strategies to plan written work*

ABC Order   Labeling

Book Report   Dramatization

Storyboards

1b *Uses strategies to draft and revise written work*

ABC Order

Labeling

1c *Uses strategies to edit and publish written work*

ABC Order

The Letter Kid

5 W's and an H

Labeling

1d *Evaluates own and others' writing*

Labeling

Book Report

5 W's and an H

1e *Dictates or writes with a logical sequence*

Teddy Bear Alphabet

Book Report

Dramatization

1f *Dictates or writes detailed descriptions of familiar persons, places, objects, or experiences*

ABC Order   Labeling

Rime Wheels   Dramatization

Favorite Part Illustration

1g *Writes in response to literature*

Labeling   Book Report

Favorite Part Illustration   Storyboards

5 W's and an H

1h *Writes in a variety of formats*

Labeling   The Letter Kid

Storyboards   5 W's and an H

Standards and Benchmarks

2 Demonstrates competence in the stylistic and rhetorical aspects of writing

2a Uses general, frequently used words to convey basic ideas

Labeling

The Letter Kid

Sound Box Cards

Book Report

5 W's and an H

3 Uses grammatical and mechanical conventions in written compositions

3a Forms letters in print and spaces words and sentences

ABC Order

Rime Wheels

Storyboards

Sound Box Cards

Draw the Room

The Letter Kid

5 W's and an H

3b Uses complete sentences

ABC Order

Rime Wheels

Dramatization

Storyboards

Labeling

Book Report

The Letter Kid

3c Uses declarative and interrogative sentences in written compositions

Labeling

The Letter Kid

5 W's and an H

ABC Order

Rime Wheels

Storyboards

3d Uses nouns in written compositions

Labeling

3e Uses verbs in written compositions

The Letter Kid

3f Uses adjectives in written compositions (e.g., uses descriptive words)

ABC Order

5 W's and an H

Labeling

3g Uses adverbs in written compositions (i.e., uses words that answer how, when, where, and why questions)

5 W's and an H

3h Uses conventions of spelling in written compositions (e.g., spells high frequency, commonly misspelled words from appropriate grade-level list; uses a dictionary and other resources to spell words; spells own first and last name)

Go Fish

Dial-Up Spelling

Ride the Word Waves

The Letter Kid

Pencil, Pen, Crayon, and Marker

Book Report

Sound Box Cards

Scavenger Hunt for Sounds

Standards and Benchmarks

3i *Uses conventions of capitalization in written compositions (e.g., first and last names, first word of a sentence)*

    ABC Order   Labeling

    Rime Wheels

3j *Uses conventions of punctuation in written compositions (e.g., uses periods after declarative sentences, uses question marks after interrogative sentences, uses commas in a series of words)*

    ABC Order   Labeling

    Rime Wheels   The Letter Kid

4 Gathers and uses information for research purposes

4a *Uses a variety of strategies to identify topics to investigate*

    Favorite Part Illustration

4b *Generates questions about topics of personal interest*

    ABC Order

    5 W's and an H

4c *Uses books to gather information for research topics*

    5 W's and an H   Favorite Part Illustration

5 Demonstrates competence in the skills and strategies of the reading process

5a *Understands that print conveys meaning*

    Draw the Room   Scavenger Hunt for Sounds

    Rime Wheels   Book Report

5b *Understands how print is organized and read*

    Counting Sounds   Word Walking

    Rime Wheels   Storyboards

5c *Creates mental images from pictures and print*

    Go Fish   Favorite Part Illustration

5d *Uses picture clues and captions to aid comprehension and to make predictions about content*

    5 W's and an H

5e *Decodes unknown words using basic elements of phonics analysis and structural analysis*

    Dial-Up Spelling   Go Fish

    Pencil, Pen, Crayon, and Marker   Ride the Word Waves

    Rime Wheels   Teddy Bear Alphabet

    Book Report   Dramatization

    Storyboards

Standards and Benchmarks

5f *Uses picture dictionary to determine word meanings*
    ABC Order   Labeling

5g *Uses self-correction strategies*
    Storyboards

5h *Reads familiar stories, poems, and passages aloud*
    Dramatization

6 Demonstrates competence in the general skills and strategies for reading a variety of literary texts

6a *Applies reading skills and strategies to a variety of familiar literary passages and texts (e.g., fairy tales, folktales, fiction, nonfiction, legends, fables, myths, poems, picture books, predictable books)*
    Book Report
    Favorite Part Illustration
    5 W's and an H
    Dramatization
    Storyboards

6b *Identifies favorite books and stories*
    Favorite Part Illustration

6c *Identifies setting, main characters, main events, and problems in stories*
    Book Report   Storyboards
    5 W's and an H

6d *Makes simple inferences regarding the order of events and possible outcomes*
    Dramatization   Storyboards
    5 W's and an H

6e *Identifies the main ideas or theme of a story*
    Dramatization   Favorite Part Illustration

6f *Relates stories to personal experiences*
    ABC Order

7 Demonstrates competence in the general skills and strategies for reading a variety of informational texts

7a *Applies reading skills and strategies to a variety of informational books*
    Favorite Part Illustration

7b *Understands the main idea of simple expository information*
    Favorite Part Illustration

7c *Summarizes information found in texts in his or her own words*
    Book Report   Dramatization
    Favorite Part Illustration   5 W's and an H

7d *Relates new information to prior knowledge and experience*
    5 W's and an H

Standards and Benchmarks

8 Demonstrates competence in speaking and listening as tools for learning

8a Recognizes the characteristic sounds and rhythms of language

Rime Wheels

8b Makes contributions in class and group discussions

Go Fish

Dramatization

8c Asks and responds to questions

Go Fish

8d Follows the rules of conversation (taking turns, staying on topic, raising hand to speak, etc.)

Go Fish

Ride the Word Waves

Dramatization

8e Uses different voice levels, phrasing, and intonation for different situations

Dramatization

8f Listens and responds to oral directions

Go Fish

Sound Box Cards

8g Listens and recites familiar stories, poems, and rhymes with patterns

Rime Wheels

8h Listens and responds to a variety of media

All Centers

Parent Support

Teaching is a partnership between teacher and child, teacher and parent, and parent and child. Parental support is an important component to effective teaching.

Each activity card lists Home Connection ideas to help the child bring the learning home. Use the letter on page 14 to advise parents of the Home Connection ideas. Simply write the suggestion in the box provided. Children can reinforce the concepts they have learned when they share homework with parents. By explaining what they are doing to others, they solidify their understanding of the skills and gain self-esteem in the process.

Technology Connections

If you have a computer available for student use, this is an excellent resource for extending and reinforcing literacy skills in the young learner. There are many interactive books currently available on CD that allow the child to hear a story read fluently and with meaningful expression. This activity builds phonemic awareness and vocabulary development as the child begins to associate the spoken word with the text on screen. Most interactive storybooks allow the child to click the mouse on a word he or she is are unsure of and hear it spoken aloud.

Even very young children can benefit from the use of a simple word processing or paint program (such as *Kid Pix*) to develop early writing skills. Simple activities that can reinforce basic literacy skills include: identifying letters of the alphabet on the keyboard; typing the beginning (or ending) letter of a word and drawing a picture to represent that word; typing a simple rebus story; or even emailing a short note to grandma! These are all great exercises to help students realize the power of the written word. A printout of any of these activities to share with others is a great source of pride as well.

Home Connection Letter

Send the following letter home with each Home Connection activity.

Date:

Dear Parents,

Your child has been busy at school learning language skills through various reading, writing, listening, and speaking activities. Purposeful practice is essential in order for your child to master these skills and be a successful reader and writer.

Please help review and reinforce our classwork by doing the following activity together with your child:

Since many experts agree that parent involvement, no matter how great or small, helps children succeed at school, we thank you for your time and effort with this valuable practice.

Sincerely,

Management

Effective center activities rely greatly on successful management. This section offers many center management suggestions. Tips on using the cards, preparing the manipulatives, and the "center" process are included here. There is no one right way to organize and integrate centers within the classroom curriculum. Often, finding what works best is a process of trial and error.

The organization and management skills needed are numerous since students work at a variety of locations and on different activities with little teacher direction. Setting expectations, using positive reinforcement, and scheduling the day are just the beginning when planning centers. There are many more tips on the next few pages that can help the teacher manage an effective literacy center classroom. Consider the following when implementing centers:

- Classroom Rules
- Acceptable Noise Level
- Grouping Students
- Location and Rotation Chart (Color Wheel)
- Limiting Center Numbers
- Monitoring Choices
- Introducing New Centers

- Changing Activities
- Managing Materials
- Literacy Center Folders
- Accountability Recording Sheets
- Using and Collecting Equipment
- Finish-Up Time
- Special Needs Students
- Transitioning Between Centers

Some teachers wish to have just a few students at each area; some choose to have a center for each student. The primary factor in this decision should be the number of students you want working at each location. Some centers may vary in the number of students who can be accommodated. One way to plan is to divide the total number of students in the class by the number of students desired at each center. For example, in a class of twenty students, four literacy centers are needed if the teacher wishes to have five children at each center.

It is important to remember to provide center activities that your class is familiar with through formal instruction. Repetition of these activities is a useful learning tool for students and necessary when mastering skills. Repetition strengthens the basic lesson for some students, while offering improvisation and extension opportunities for others.

Literacy Center time should be a fundamental part of the instructional day for each student. They should not simply be used as a reward for finishing a particular task or good behavior. All students should avail themselves of center activities.

How To Rotate Centers

Productive and effective center activities rely greatly on successful management. This section will provide the teacher with center management suggestions. Tips on dividing your students into groups and center rotation are included in this section. It is important to note that teachers must operate centers in a way that best suits their style, classroom, and students. Below are several suggestions for running a literacy center environment.

Scheduling

The first step in implementing literacy learning centers is scheduling. Decide how much time of the instructional day will be devoted to centers. Once that block of time has been established, the number of centers that a student will visit each day can be determined. The average learning center takes about fifteen minutes to complete. Remember to adjust the time to fit the developmental needs of your students. An average day consists of two to four centers in a rotation. It is conceivable that a center task could be too challenging or not challenging enough for your students. You may need to adjust the centers to fit your students' needs. Keep in mind, not only are your students' working on literacy, they are also working on language and social skills while working at the centers.

Groups

Next, you need to develop a plan for dividing your children into groups. Primary children relate well to and recognize colors. For example, divide your students into three groups, a green group, a blue group, and a red group. Then, rotate your color groups through the centers. Remember to keep in mind the number of children you want working in a center at a time, and the dynamics of each group. You may want to put a few academically strong children in a group with a few academically challenged children. A group configured this way would enable you to move around the room to observe more freely, or work with a small group, rather than spending the bulk of your time assisting a group that consists of all academically challenged students. Encourage your students to work together and discuss the center with each other. Tell them that if they have questions, to first try and work it out as a group and second, come find you, the teacher.

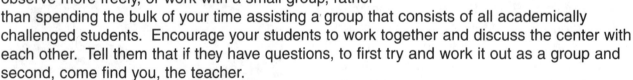

One last tip to help you successfully implement literacy centers into your classroom—**LET GO!** During this valuable time, students are engaged in practicing skills and strategies that they have already been taught. Generally, the teacher will not be instructing, but monitoring and facilitating. Students will be practicing previously taught skills, working to solve problems, and teaching each other. Sit back, observe, and take notes while your students learn.

Implementing Activity Cards

The primary concept behind *Literacy Centers for Reading Skills (Pre K–1)* is that the centers provide independent practice. There are approximately six literacy center activities per category. Each activity is presented in several steps. First, present the activity as a directed whole-group activity or as a directed small-group activity. Then, present it as an official literacy center. Share the components, the process, and how to put the center away when finished.

Ease of use is at the core of a good center. The cards are simple and straightforward. Step-by-step instructions are provided describing how to prepare each center. The student cards can be laminated for durability. They provide simple, clear directions with illustrations. Ideally, the teacher will have instructed the students numerous times on how to perform the center activity. The student card will serve as a reminder for the student. The student card is not intended for use as instruction for a child who has not received prior instruction from a teacher. Each center must be taught (modeled) prior to its implementation in order to ensure future mastery of the skill being practiced. The teacher page consists of the following elements:

Objective

Each lesson has an objective for the area of practice.

What You Will Need

The materials required for the activity are listed here. Details are given on what needs to be purchased or made as far as manipulatives are concerned. Every effort has been made to provide as many finished, ready-to-use, materials as possible in an effort to limit teacher prep time. Reproducible, blackline masters are provided. Many are open-ended to provide flexibility to best suit your curriculum and student ability levels. **Note:** When the term *any text* is listed in the materials list, teachers should provide students with appropriate reading material. Choose from an anthology story, a basal reader, a decodable book, or a weekly periodical such as *TIME for Kids*.

Create It

The Create It section provides simple instructions on the few steps necessary to create each center activity.

Teach It

A directed lesson for each activity is included. Often, scripted words to present the lesson to the group are given in italics. The lesson is to teach the activity and is not intended as a lesson that teaches the literacy concept that is to be practiced. Centers should reinforce previously taught concepts. Model the center activity for the students more than once.

There is no mandatory or steadfast order in which to introduce the centers into your classroom. The activities should be chosen based on the literacy needs of your students and the curriculum areas you are currently teaching the students.

The Literacy Center Folder

The utilization of a literacy center folder for each child is an effective management tool in the implementation of daily, independent practice time. Folders can be used to track which centers students have visited. They can also be used to assess students' completion of the center and progress toward mastery. One of the most efficient ways to store these large literacy center folders in the classroom is with the use of rectangular, plastic laundry baskets.

When introducing the centers, encourage students to place completed worksheets in the front of their folders. Periodically, remind students to place their most recent work in the front of the file.

These literacy center folders offer the teacher a glimpse of each child as an individual, taking into consideration learning style, developmental stage, interests, and progress. Teachers can check the contents of folders on a daily or weekly basis to hold students accountable. The forms of assessment and the extent to which completion and correctness are "graded" are completely at the teacher's discretion.

Student accountability can vary from recording responses extensively to a self-check, or quick peer check with no written response at all. Since some activities have recording tasks built into them, while others do not, literacy center folders make management of student work easy.

The time when teachers themselves need to check student work for correctness is when students are being tested or checked for mastery. Teachers should evaluate and "authentically assess" tests and one-on-one performance assignments, rather than daily practice work. These evaluations should be done after sufficient instruction and practice time in which students can check and correct their errors.

Organizing & Storing

The activity centers presented in this book can be stored in a multitude of ways. Self-sealing plastic baggies in the gallon size seem to provide the most protection from damage and the risk of losing activity components. The bags can be labeled with permanent markers and stored in boxes or plastic tubs.

Sight Words Centers

100 Most Frequently Used Words

Sight Word Cards*

Word Walking

ABC Order

Go Fish

Pencil, Pen, Crayon, and Marker

Ride the Word Waves

Dial-Up Spelling

*Sight Word Cards can be used with a variety of centers.

Notes

100 Most Frequently Used Words

Sight Words 1–50

1–25	26–50
the	or
of	one
and	had
a	by
to	words
in	but
is	not
you	what
that	all
it	were
he	we
was	when
for	your
on	can
are	said
as	there
with	use
his	an
they	each
I	which
at	she
be	do
this	how
have	their
from	if

100 Most Frequently Used Words

Sight Words 51–100

51–75

will
up
other
about
out
many
then
them
these
so
some
her
would
make
like
him
into
time
has
look
two
more
write
go
see

76–100

number
no
way
could
people
my
than
first
water
been
call
who
am
its
now
find
long
down
day
did
get
come
made
may
part

the	**in**
of	**is**
and	**you**
a	**that**
to	**it**

Sight Words   Sight Words

Sight Words   Sight Words

Sight Words   Sight Words

Sight Words   Sight Words

Sight Words   Sight Words

he

as

was

with

for

his

on

they

are

I

Sight Words

Sight Words

Sight Words

Sight Words

Sight Words

Sight Words

Sight Words

Sight Words

Sight Words

Sight Words

at	or
be	one
this	had
have	by
from	words

Sight Words   Sight Words

Sight Words   Sight Words

Sight Words   Sight Words

Sight Words   Sight Words

Sight Words   Sight Words

but	**we**
not	**when**
what	**your**
all	**can**
were	**said**

Sight Words   **Sight Words**

Sight Words   **Sight Words**

Sight Words   **Sight Words**

Sight Words   **Sight Words**

Sight Words   **Sight Words**

there	**she**
use	**do**
an	**how**
each	**their**
which	**if**

Sight Words　　　Sight Words

Sight Words　　　Sight Words

Sight Words　　　Sight Words

Sight Words　　　Sight Words

Sight Words　　　Sight Words

will

many

up

then

other

them

about

these

out

so

Sight Words   Sight Words

Sight Words   Sight Words

Sight Words   Sight Words

Sight Words   Sight Words

Sight Words   Sight Words

some	him
would	time
her	into
make	has
like	look

Sight Words   **Sight Words**

Sight Words   **Sight Words**

Sight Words   **Sight Words**

Sight Words   **Sight Words**

Sight Words   **Sight Words**

two	**number**
more	**no**
write	**way**
go	**could**
see	**people**

Sight Words   Sight Words

Sight Words   Sight Words

Sight Words   Sight Words

Sight Words   Sight Words

Sight Words   Sight Words

my

call

than

who

first

am

water

its

been

now

Sight Words   Sight Words

Sight Words   Sight Words

Sight Words   Sight Words

Sight Words   Sight Words

Sight Words   Sight Words

find	get
long	come
down	made
day	may
did	part

Sight Words   Sight Words

Sight Words   Sight Words

Sight Words   Sight Words

Sight Words   Sight Words

Sight Words   Sight Words

Word Walking

Objective: Provides independent practice reading Instant Sight Words.

What You Will Need

- laminated Footprint Word Cards
- 100 Most Frequently Used Words (pages 21–22)

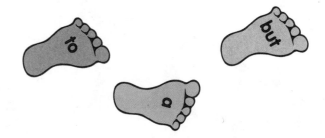

Create It

1. Make copies of the feet. Write the words you wish to teach, one word per foot. Make certain you write each word on a foot in the same place, going in the same direction.

2. Laminate the Footprint Word Cards, cut them out and place them in a bag.

Note: If you plan to reuse the feet with different words, laminate them first and use permanent marker to write the words on the laminate. You can to use hairspray to erase the words.

Teach It

Today we are going on a "word walk." I am going to place these footprints on the floor and we are going to walk on them. You will read and say each word as you step on it. Let's get started.

Do this lesson with your students until you are confident that they are able to do the center procedures independently.

Teacher Tips

- Be sure to include both left and right feet! Write the words across the balls of the feet.
- Use silly slippers, like animal characters, or big fuzzy ones, to encourage the "reader" to move more slowly and keep his or her eyes on the print. This will clearly identify which student is the "reader."
- Have students reshuffle and redistribute the feet and walk again after everyone has had a turn to be the "reader."

Keep in Mind: Laminated feet can be slippery. You may wish to glue squares of sandpaper or rubber matting to the back of each footprint.

Extension Idea

- As students step on a word, have them use the word in a sentence.

Home Connection: Provide students with an "at home" set of footprints by reducing the size of the footprint pattern.

Word Walking

Footprints

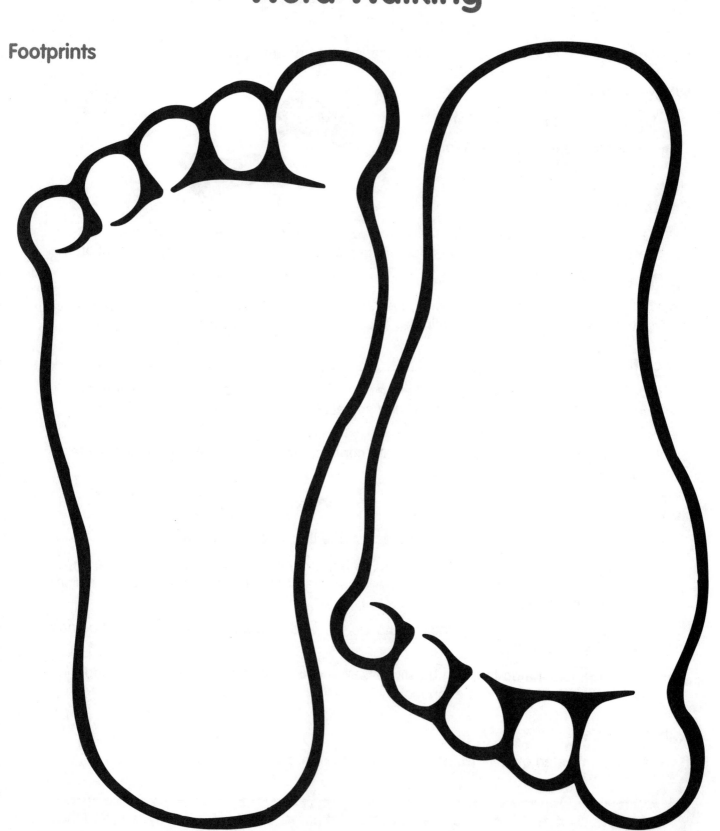

Word Walking

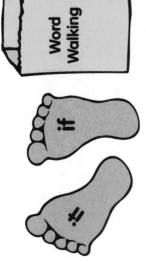

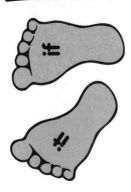

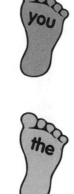

1. Take the feet out of the bag.

2. Lay the feet on the floor like a path. (Left/Right)

3. Make sure the words are facing up.

4. Take turns and walk along the feet, one at a time, and say each word as you step on it.

ABC Order

Objective: Provides independent practice reading sight words in addition to the alphabetizing skill.

What You Will Need

- selected Sight Word Cards (pages 23–42)
- ABC Order (pages 51–54) or strip
- ABC Order recording sheet (page 48)
- writing tools

Create It

1. Provide the items above in a center.
2. Determine if the Alphabet Chart should be cut up to form a continuous strip for the learning center or left as a chart. If a strip is desired, prepare the strip by cutting the chart into strips and gluing the ends together. Laminate the strip for durability.
3. If an alphabet chart is to be created, connect pages 51 and 53 and laminate.
4. Copy the appropriate number of ABC Order recording sheets for your students.

Teach It

This center can be used continuously by changing the words to be studied. *Today we are going to put some of our sight words in ABC order. This is called "alphabetizing."* Display the word you have chosen. *Let's look at the first letter of each word. Which of these words begins with a letter that comes at the beginning of the alphabet? Look at the chart if you need help. Which first letter of what word comes first in the alphabet?* Help children find the word that would come first when alphabetizing. Explain to your students the procedure when two or more words have the same first letter. *If words have the same first letter, look at the second letter to decide where it belongs in the alphabetized list. Let's try a few together.* With the assistance of the students, place the cards in alphabetical order. Write the words on the ABC Order Recording Sheet (page 48) when you have them in order.

Do this lesson with your students until you are confident they are able to do the center independently.

Teacher Tip

- Alphabetizing words by the second or third letter can become tricky. Try to choose words that have different beginning letters when initiating this activity.

Keep in Mind: Students must be taught the concept of alphabetizing first. Discuss with your students the idea that the alphabet is always in the same order, it never changes.

Extension Ideas

- Use weekly spelling, vocabulary, or thematic word lists instead of the sight words.
- Modify the number of words to be alphabetized.

Home Connection: Have students do this activity at home with a parent, using a list of words you have provided.

ABC Order

Directions: Write the words you have chosen in alphabetical order.

_____   _____

_____   _____

_____   _____

_____   _____

_____   _____

_____   _____

_____   _____

_____   _____

_____   _____

_____   _____

_____   _____

_____   _____

_____   _____

_____   _____

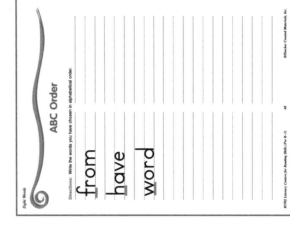

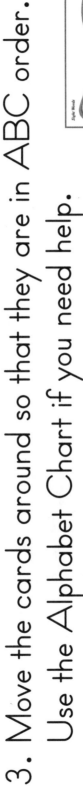

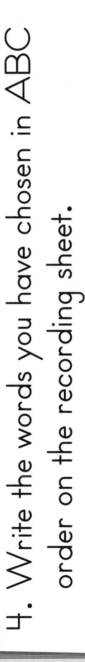

ABC Order

1. Read the word cards.

2. Look at the first letter in each word.

3. Move the cards around so that they are in ABC order.
Use the Alphabet Chart if you need help.

4. Write the words you have chosen in ABC order on the recording sheet.

5. Underline the first letter of each word.

Go Fish

Objective: Provides independent practice in the area of reading sight words.

What You Will Need

- Go Fish Cards
- list of sight words to be studied
- markers

Create It

1. Write each word to be studied on two Go Fish cards.
2. Laminate the cards.

Note: If you plan to reuse the fish cards with different words, laminate them first and use permanent marker to write the words on the laminate. You can use hairspray to erase the words and write new ones.

Teach It

Today we are going to play a card game called "Go Fish." The main idea is for each player to get as many pairs of words as they can. A "pair" is a set of two cards that match. You will each pick five cards and hold them in your hand so no one else can see them. The rest of the cards will stay in the middle of the table face down. Those cards will be in the "pond."

Take out any pairs in your hand and lay each pair down in front of you. When it is your turn, you will ask another player if he or she has a word card that you need to make a pair. If they do, they will give their card to you. If they don't have the card, they will tell you to "Go Fish" and you will need to draw a card from the "Go Fish Pond." Then, it is the other student's turn.

Do these lessons with your students until you are confident that they are able to do the center procedures independently.

Teacher Tips

- Have children lay the cards face-up in front of them if holding them in their hands is too difficult.
- Have students play Go Fish the traditional way first, using number cards.

Keep in Mind: Students may need to be reminded of the proper way to take turns while playing a game.

Extension Ideas

- Use weekly spelling lists instead of sight words.
- Modify the number of words or cards.

Home Connection: Have students make a set of cards to use at home. Supply blank cards and a list of words to be practiced.

Go Fish Cards

  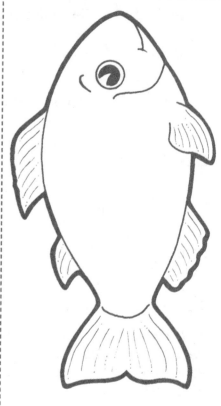

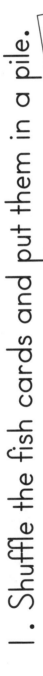

Go Fish

1. Shuffle the fish cards and put them in a pile.

2. Take turns taking 5 cards each.

3. Match all the pairs you have in your hand.

4. Take turns asking another player if he or she has a match for one of the cards in your hand.

5. Take the card from the player who has it or "Go Fish."

6. "Go Fish" in the pile in the middle.

7. Keep playing until all the cards have been paired.

Pencil, Pen, Crayon, and Marker

Objective: Provides independent practice reading and writing sight words.

What You Will Need

- four frozen juice cans cleaned and with no sharp edges
- list of sight words to be studied
- Pencil, Pen, Crayon, and Marker recording sheet (page 60)
- pencils, pens, crayons, and markers

Create It

1. Fill each of the four juice cans with a different writing tool. Arrange the containers in the center of the work area.
2. Supply copies of the Pencil, Pen, Crayon, and Marker recording sheet for students.

Teach It

Students write the sight words using various writing tools. This center can be used continuously by changing the words to be studied. Introduce the center and the materials. Explain the process. *Today we are going to practice writing sight words. We will write each sight word on the list four times. Each time we will use a different writing tool to write the word.* Do this lesson with your students until you are confident they are able to do the center independently.

Teacher Tip

- The greater the assortment of writing tools you provide, the more fun this center becomes for the student.

Keep in Mind: Choose writing tools that are washable. You may wish to take precautions to protect clothing.

Extension Ideas

- Use weekly spelling lists instead of sight word lists.
- Have students layer the words on top of each other to create a word picture: pen over pencil, crayon over pen, and marker over the crayon.
- Create a work of "word-art." Use glue to write the words and cover the glue with glitter, or change the color of glue by mixing it with various colors of tempera paint. Have students write the words in the colored glue and set the paper aside to dry.

Home Connection: Have students do this project as homework with a list of words you have provided. Encourage them to use as many different writing tools as possible for each word. The child could then use chalk to write the words on the sidewalk or patio.

Pencil, Pen, Crayon, and Marker

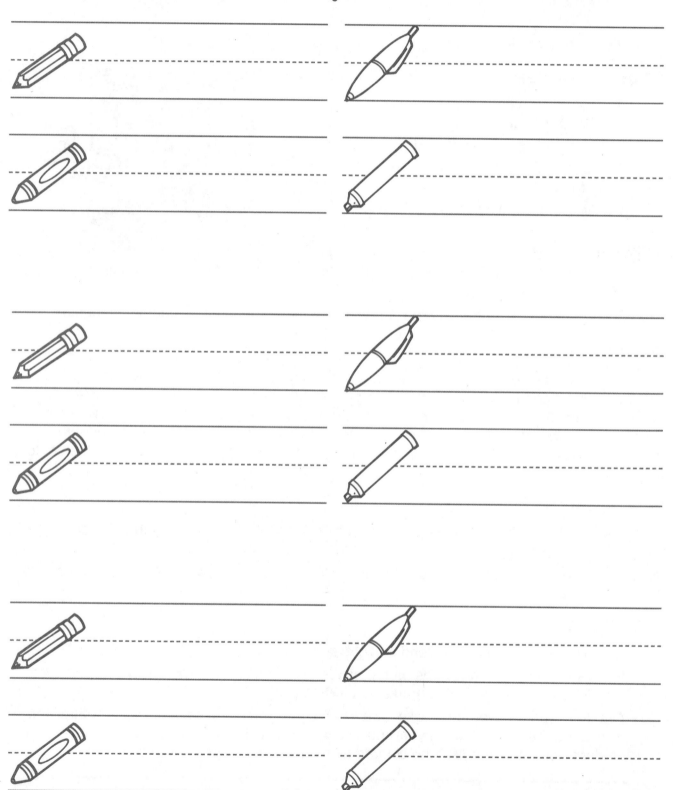

Pencil, Pen, Crayon, and Marker

1. Read the first word on the list.

2. Write the word with a pencil.

3. Write the word again with a pen.

4. Write the word again with a crayon.

5. Finally, write the word with a marker.

6. Do the same thing for each word on the list.

Ride the Word Waves

Objective: Provides independent practice reading sight words.

What You Will Need

- blue poster board
- markers
- hole punch
- paper clips
- index cards
- craft stick or small toy surfboard
- Ride the Word Waves cards (pages 67–75)

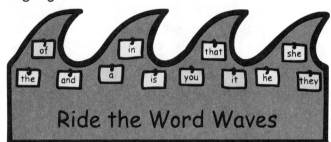

Create It

1. Write the words to be studied on the index cards strips.
2. Using the marker, draw a large wave across the blue poster board.
3. Punch small holes into the board. Space the holes evenly across the wave.
4. Slide one end of a paper clip through each hole.
5. Hang the index card strips from the paper clips.
6. Provide a "surfboard" (tracker) at the center.

Teach It

This center allows students to travel by "surfing" or "riding" the waves as they read sight words. *Today we are going to Ride the Word Waves while we read the sight words. Each person at this center will take turns riding his or her surfboard over the waves, reading each word as he or she goes. If you miss a word, you "wipe out" and need to start at the beginning when it is your turn again. Later, you can surf some of the Ride the Word Waves Cards on pages 64–75 or create new ones using the templates on page 64.*

Do this lesson with your students until you are confident they are able to do the center independently.

Teacher Tip

- A lot of different items could be used as a surfboard. Many novelty catalogues sell surfboard key chains that would work well. You could also provide each student with his or her own personalized surfboard (craft stick) for this activity.

Keep in Mind: Students may take advantage of this center to highlight the aspect of wiping out on the waves rather than reading the words. Encourage children to avoid "wiping out."

Extension Ideas

- Instead of riding the waves, children could "climb the mountain" and pretend that they are rock climbing and need to start at the beginning after belaying down on their rope.

Home Connection: Send home a copy of one of the Ride the Word Waves Strips found on pages 67–75, along with a "surfboard" to play the game with a family member.

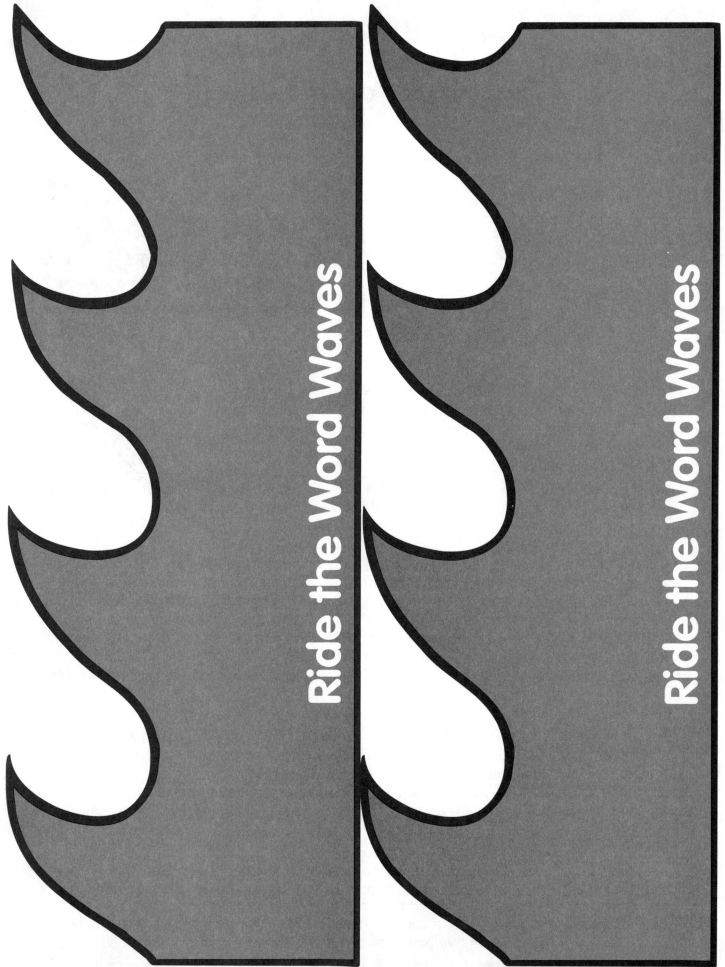

Ride the Word Waves

Ride the Word Waves

64

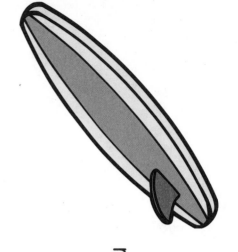

Ride the Word Waves

1. Using the surfboard, surf along the wave card.

2. Read each word as you get to it.

3. You "wipe out" if you miss a word. Then, you must start at the beginning of the Ride the Word Wave Card.

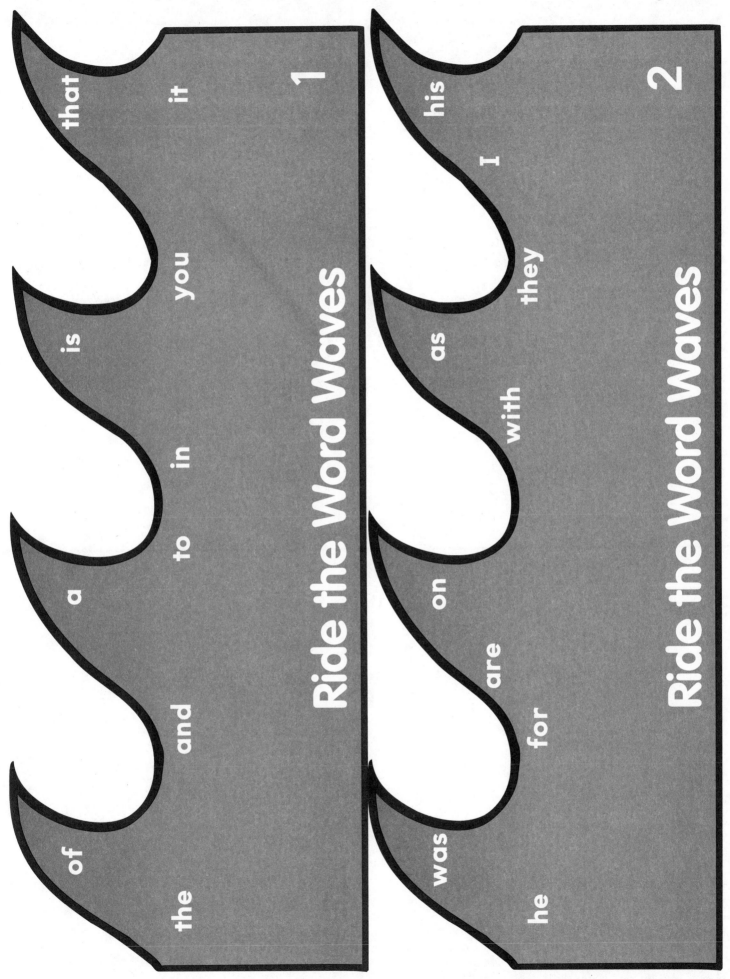

Ride the Word Waves

1

that
it
you
is
in
to
a
and
of
the

Ride the Word Waves

2

his
I
they
as
with
on
are
for
was
he

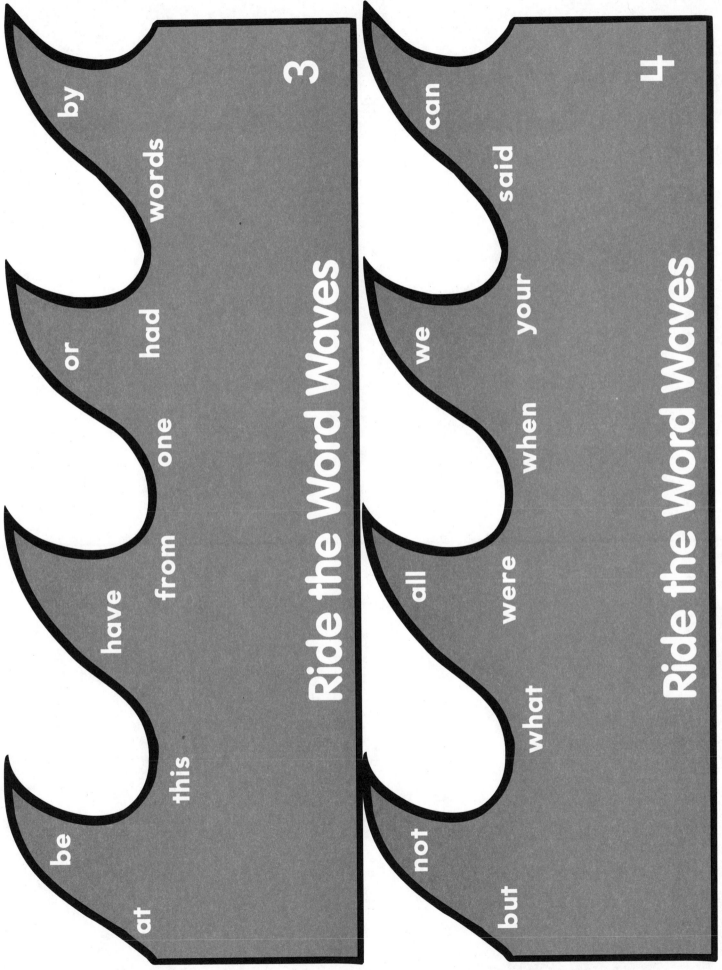

3

by

words

had

or

one

from

have

this

be

at

Ride the Word Waves

4

can

said

your

we

when

were

all

what

not

but

Ride the Word Waves

#3702 Literacy Centers for Reading Skills (Pre K–1)

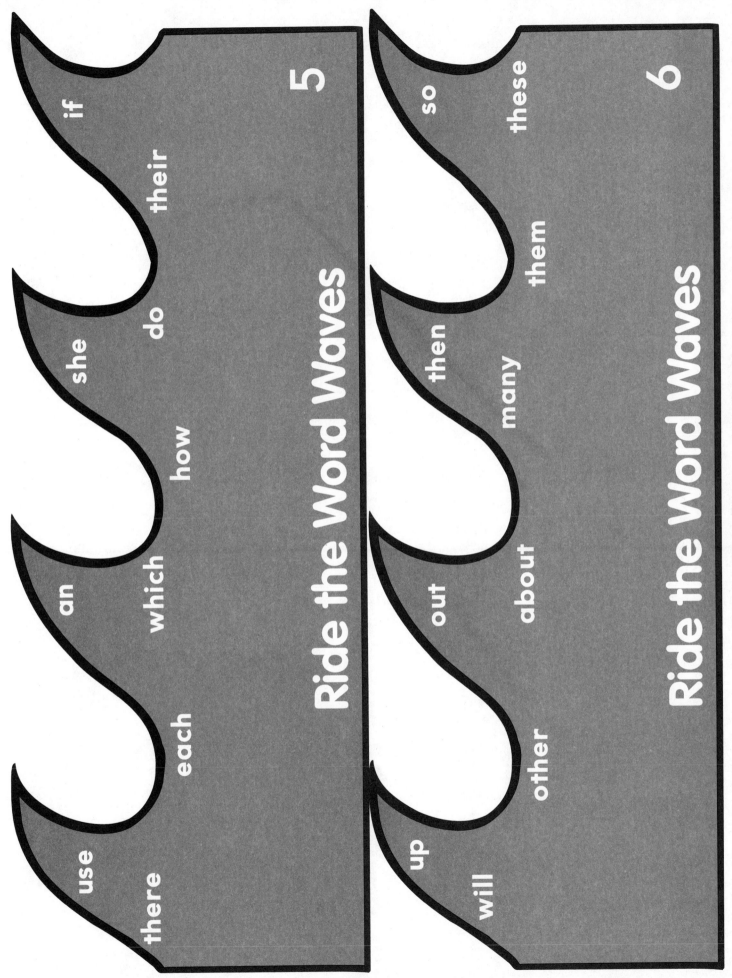

Ride the Word Waves

5

if
their
do
she
how
an
which
each
use
there

Ride the Word Waves

6

so
these
them
then
many
about
out
other
up
will

7

look
has
time
him
into
like
make
would
her
some

Ride the Word Waves

8

way
people
no
could
number
go
see
write
two
more

Ride the Word Waves

Ride the Word Waves

9

its
now
who
am
been
call
water
first
my
than

Ride the Word Waves

10

may
part
made
get
come
did
down
long
day
find

Dial-Up Spelling

Objective: Provides independent practice in the area of sight word spelling.

What You Will Need

- Telephone Card (page 81)
- copies of the Dial-Up Spelling recording sheet (page 78)
- pencils
- Sight Word Cards (pages 23–42)

Create It

1. Laminate the Telephone Card for durability (optional).
2. Provide students with 5 to 10 sight words to be practiced.
3. Provide students with copies of the recording sheet.

Teach It

Students use a copy of a telephone keypad to create a code for the sight words to be studied. *Today we are going to create a telephone number for a few of our sight words.* Hold up a Sight Word Card. Ask for volunteers to read the word. Using the sounds represented, establish with all of the students the word on the card. Write the word on a recording sheet. *Now we are going to create a code for this word using the telephone keypad.* Show the students the Telephone Card. *Do you see that each number key, except for 1 and 0, lists different letters of the alphabet? We can make number codes for our sight words using this card. Watch.* Write the corresponding number for the sight word using the keypad code.

Do this lesson with your students until you are confident that they are able to do the center procedures independently.

Teacher Tip

- Remind students that they should never randomly press buttons with a real connected phone.

Keep in Mind: Students will need to be reminded that the *Oper* on 0 is not part of the code. The letters Q and Z are not found on a traditional telephone keypad. They are assigned here to ease confusion with young children.

Extension Idea

- Use weekly spelling lists instead of sight words.

My Spelling Words	
one	four
two	five
three	six

Home Connection: Have students do this project as homework with a list of words you provide them. Instruct students to use a copy of the phonecard to come up with telephone codes for the new words.

Dial-Up Spelling

Word   **Code**

1. ___was___   ___927___

2. _____   _____

3. _____   _____

4. _____   _____

5. _____   _____

6. _____   _____

7. _____   _____

Dial-Up Spelling

that

was

to

1. Select a Sight Word Card.

2. Write the word on the recording sheet.

927
_____

8428
_____

was
- - - - - - -

that
- - - - - - -

3. Use the Telephone Card to make a code number for the word.

Dial-Up Spelling

Telephone Card

Phonics and Decoding Centers

Rime Wheels

Labeling

Teddy Bear Alphabet

Draw the Room

Sound Box Cards

Scavenger Hunt for Sounds

Notes

Rime Wheels

Objective: Provides independent practice in the area of onset and rime.

What You Will Need

- Rime Wheel Cards for rime and onset to be practiced.
- copies of Rime wheels recording sheet
- pencils
- brads
- scissors

Create It

1. Laminate the Rime Wheel Cards for durability (optional).
2. Cut out the two parts of the Rime Wheel.
3. Cut out the square on the rime wheel noted by the dashed line on the front part of the wheel.
4. Press a brad through the center of the onset and rime wheels to connect them.

Note: If creating your own Rime Wheel, be careful that onsets are not included that could result in unacceptable words.

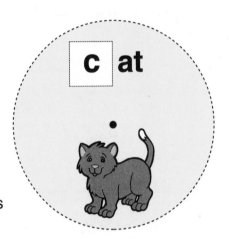

Teach It

Students will practice blending onsets and rimes. *Today we are going to make several words using a Rime Wheel. Look at the wheel.* (Cover the onset and show students the rime.) *What sound do these letters make?* Have students volunteer the answer. Sound out the letters to establish the correct answer. *All of the words that you can make with the wheel will rhyme since they have the same ending.* After the rime is established, uncover the window and read the word created by adding the onset. *Write the word that has been built. Draw a picture of the word on the recording sheet. Continue to spin the wheel and record pictures of the words created.* This lesson and center activity should be done after working with the rime pattern in other lessons as well. Do this lesson with your students until you are confident that they are able to do the center procedures independently.

Teacher Tip

- Sometimes the words are not something for which a picture can be drawn. In that case, write the word only.

Keep in Mind: It is important to allign the two wheels correctly before pressing in the brad.

Home Connection: Read books containing rhyming text. Try Dr. Seuss books or other poetry collections. Encourage children to identify rhyming words.

Rime Wheels

Activity Sheet

Directions: Write the words you made on your Rime Wheel on the lines below. Whenever possible, draw a picture of the word.

1.

2.

3.

4.

Rime Wheels

c at

c + at = cat

1. Turn the wheel.

2. Read the word.

3. Write the word.

cat

4. Draw a picture of the word.

Rime Wheels

Rime Wheel

ip

Rime Wheels

Onset Wheel

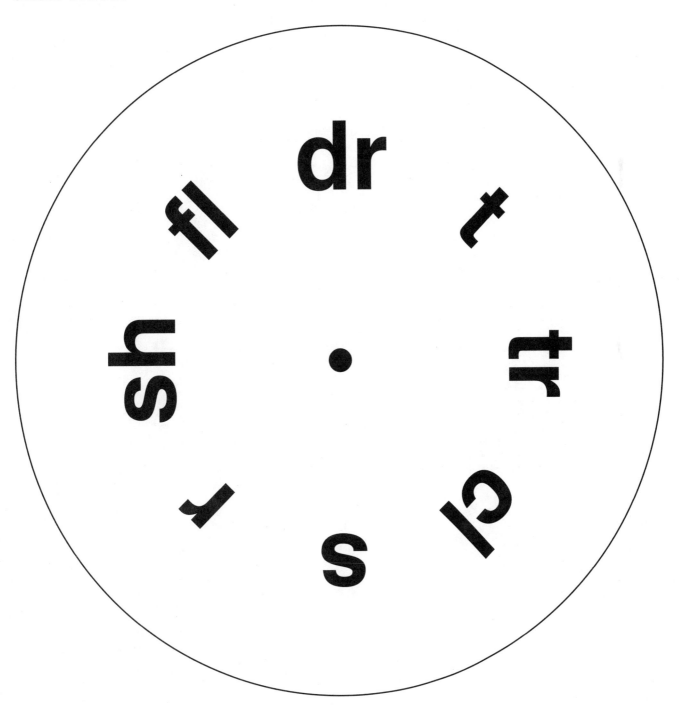

Use with page 97.

Rime Wheels

Rime Wheel

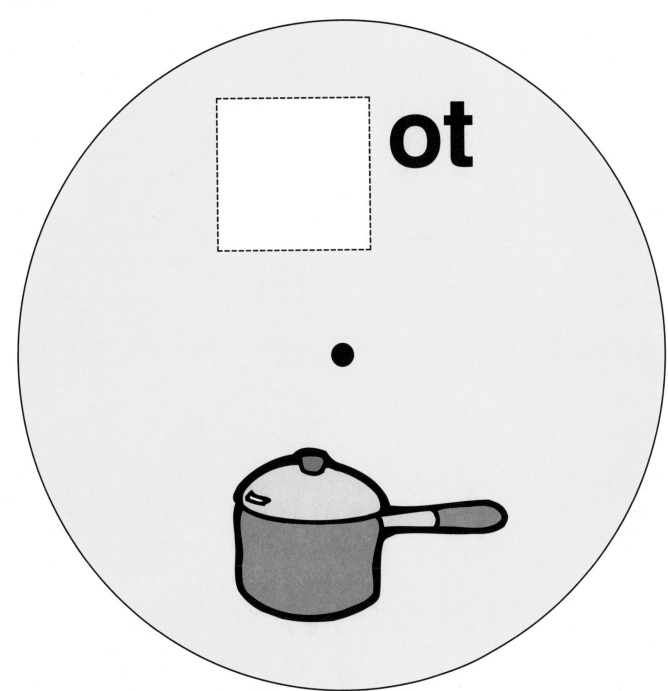

Rime Wheels

Onset Wheel

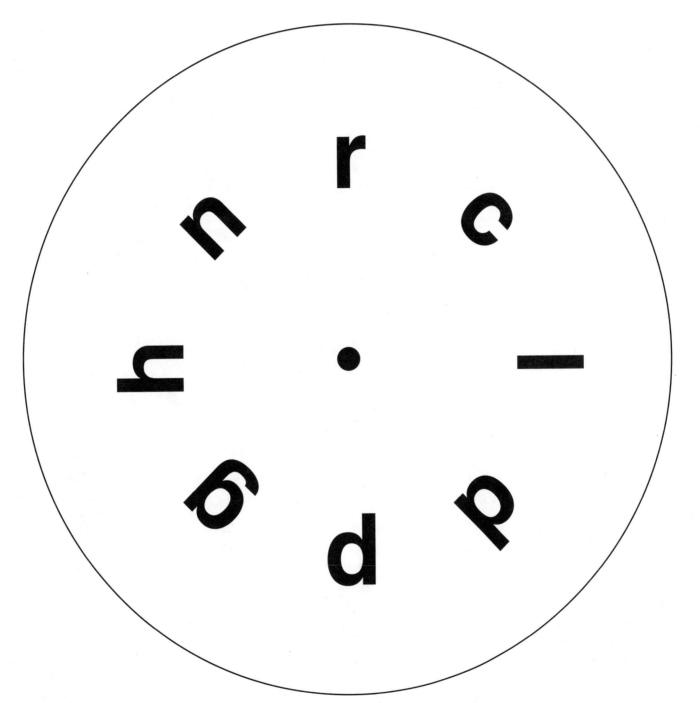

Use with page 101.

Rime Wheels

Rime Wheel

ing

Rime Wheels

Onset Wheel

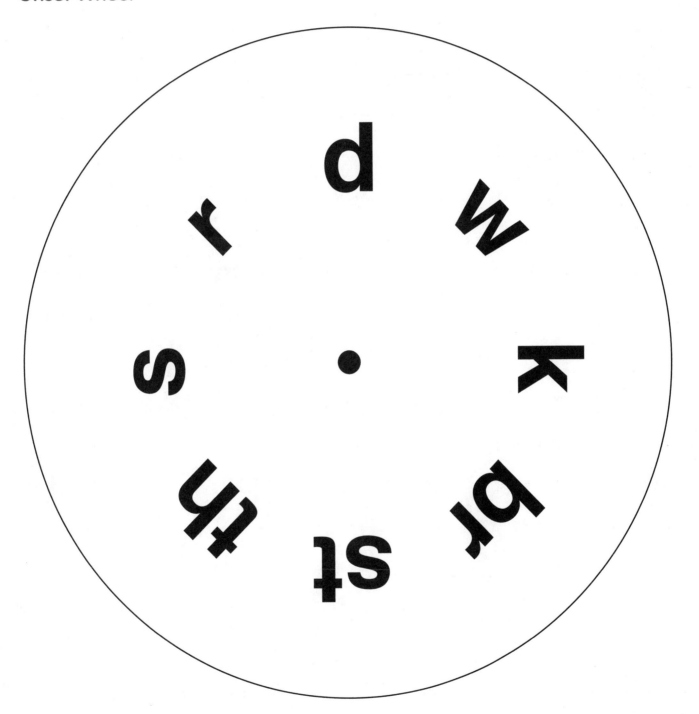

Use with page 105.

Rime Wheels

Blank Rime Wheel

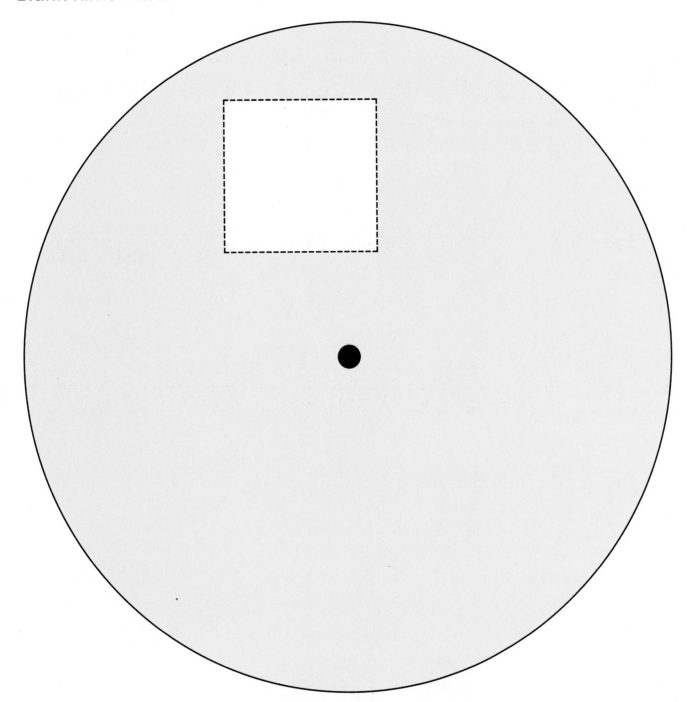

Labeling

Objective: Provides independent practice in the area of word decoding and phonics.

What You Will Need

- Labeling Cards (pages 115, 117, 119)
- damp cloths or wipes
- erasable pens (overhead markers)

Create It

1. Cut out the Labeling Cards. Enlarge them if possible.
2. Laminate the cards.
3. Arrange the pictures, erasable pens, and damp clothes or wipes in the literacy center.

Teach It

Students will label pictures of known items. *Today we are going to label pictures. Remember, when we spell words, it is very important to listen to every sound we hear. Write down the sounds you hear.* Say the word slowly and listen for sounds. *Start with the beginning sound, then the middle sounds. Finally, write the ending sound.*

Demonstrate to students how to label the parts of a picture. Show how even one item, such as a bike, can be labeled even further—pedal, seat, wheel, etc. Encourage children to write as many descriptive words as possible.

Do this lesson with your students until you are confident that they are able to do the center procedures independently.

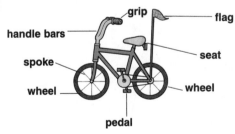

Teacher Tips

- For additional labeling cards, attach pictures, clip art, shape pads, or other items onto cardstock or construction paper and laminate them. Have children label them with overhead markers and erase the cards when finished.

Keep in Mind: Some students really dislike having to erase their work. Accept invented spelling on this activity. The primary focus is on sounds, especially initial and ending sounds.

Extension Idea

- Encourage students to make their own pictures and label them.

Home Connection: Have students draw a picture of their rooms at home. Instruct students to label the items in their drawings.

Labeling

1. Select a picture to label.

2. Label as many things as you can.

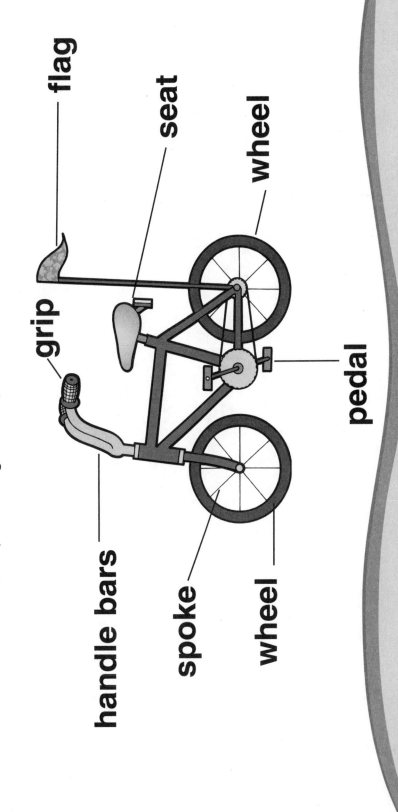

flag

seat

wheel

grip

pedal

handle bars

spoke

wheel

Labeling

Labeling

Labeling

Teddy Bear Alphabet

Objective: Provides independent practice for letter identification and letter order.

What You Will Need

- Teddy Bear Alphabet Cards (pages 125–130)
- Teddy Bear Alphabet recording sheet (page 122)

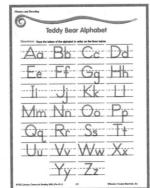

Create It

1. Cut apart the Teddy Bear Alphabet cards.
2. Make copies of the Teddy Bear Alphabet recording sheet.

Teach It

Today we are going to put the alphabet cards in order. *I have the "A" card, which is first. The front of the card has the uppercase letter. The back of the card has the lowercase letter.* Distribute the various teddy bear cards to the children. *Look at your cards and say the letter to yourself. I am going to put the "A" down here. When I call the next letter, the person who is holding it may come up and place the card in order.*

When we finish laying out all 26 letters, we will go back and say the sounds they make. Then, we will trace the letters of the alphabet in order on the recording sheet.

Do this lesson with your students until you are confident they are able to do the center independently.

Teacher Tips

- Provide a lot of floor space for this activity. Give students time and room to work with all the cards.
- Specify whether you want students to use uppercase or lowercase letters.

Keep in Mind: Some letters make more than one sound. Letters for example, the letter "C" makes a hard and soft sound. Provide examples of words that use both sounds.

Extension Idea

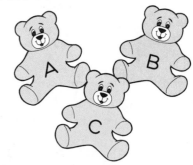

- Hand out the alphabet cards to your students. Ask each student to tell what letter comes before or after the letter he or she is holding, when it is his or her turn.

- Hand out all the cards in random order. Have the students arrange themselves in alphabetical order, using the cards.

Home Connection: Have the students draw a picture of something in their house for each of the letters/sounds.

Teddy Bear Alphabet

Directions: Trace the letters of the alphabet in order on the lines below.

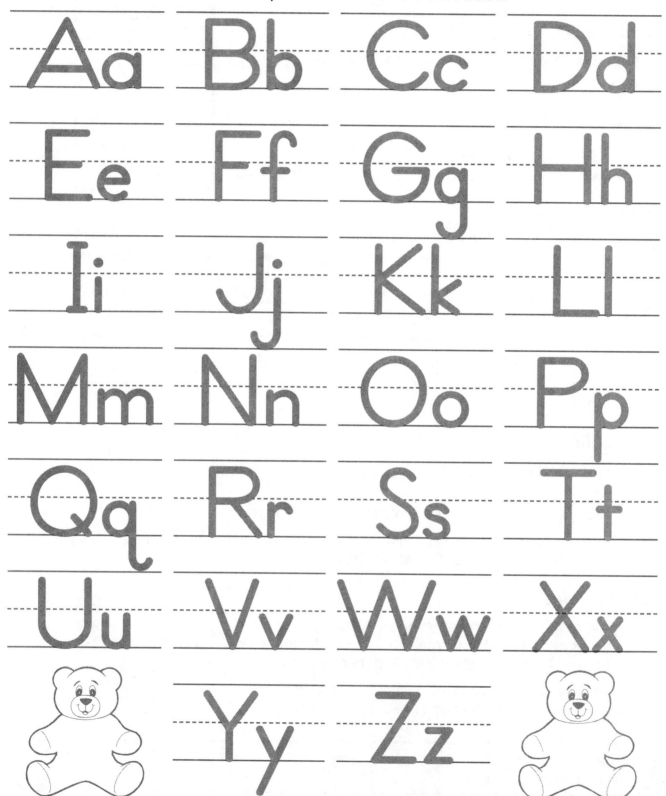

Teddy Bear Alphabet

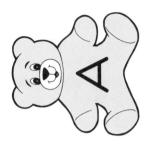
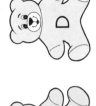

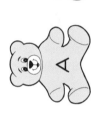

1. Lay the cards out and identify each letter.

2. Find the "A" card.

3. Find the next letter in the alphabet and lay it next to the "A."

4. Continue placing the letters in order until you get to "Z."

5. Say each letter and the sound each letter makes.

6. Trace the letters on the Teddy Bear Alphabet Sheet.

Teddy Bear Alphabet Cards

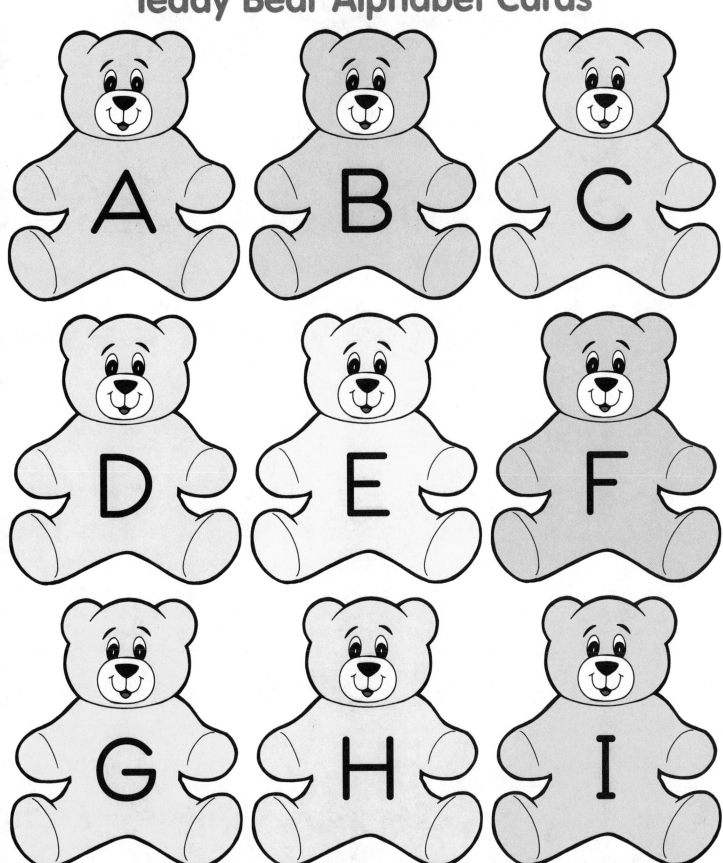

Teddy Bear Alphabet Cards

c   b   a

f   e   d

i   h   g

Teddy Bear Alphabet Cards

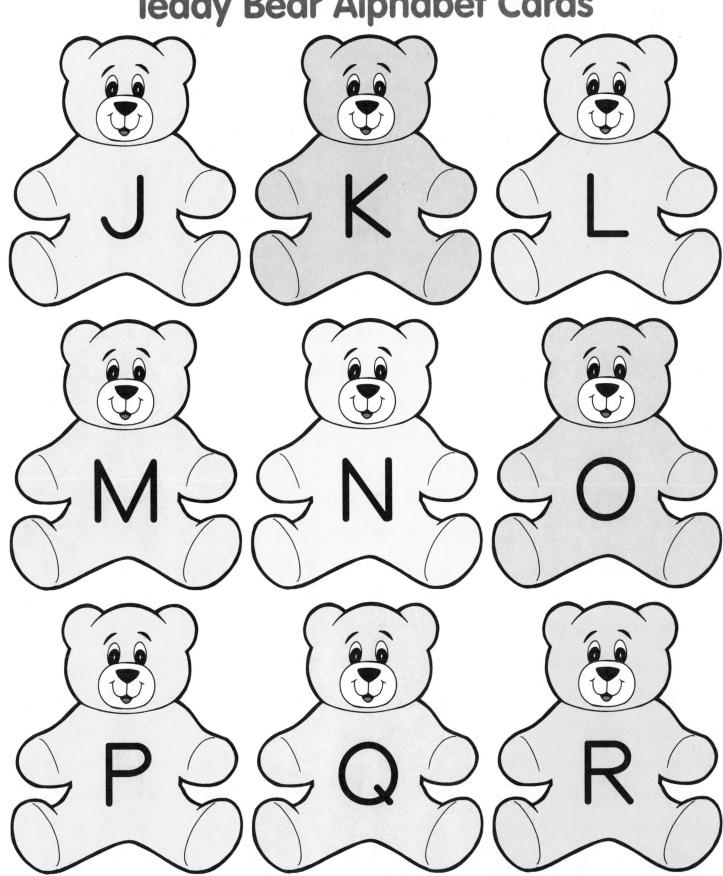

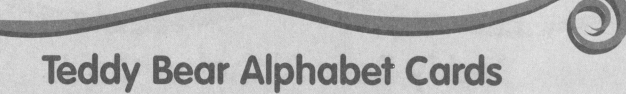

Teddy Bear Alphabet Cards

l   k   j

o   n   m

r   q   p

Teddy Bear Alphabet Cards

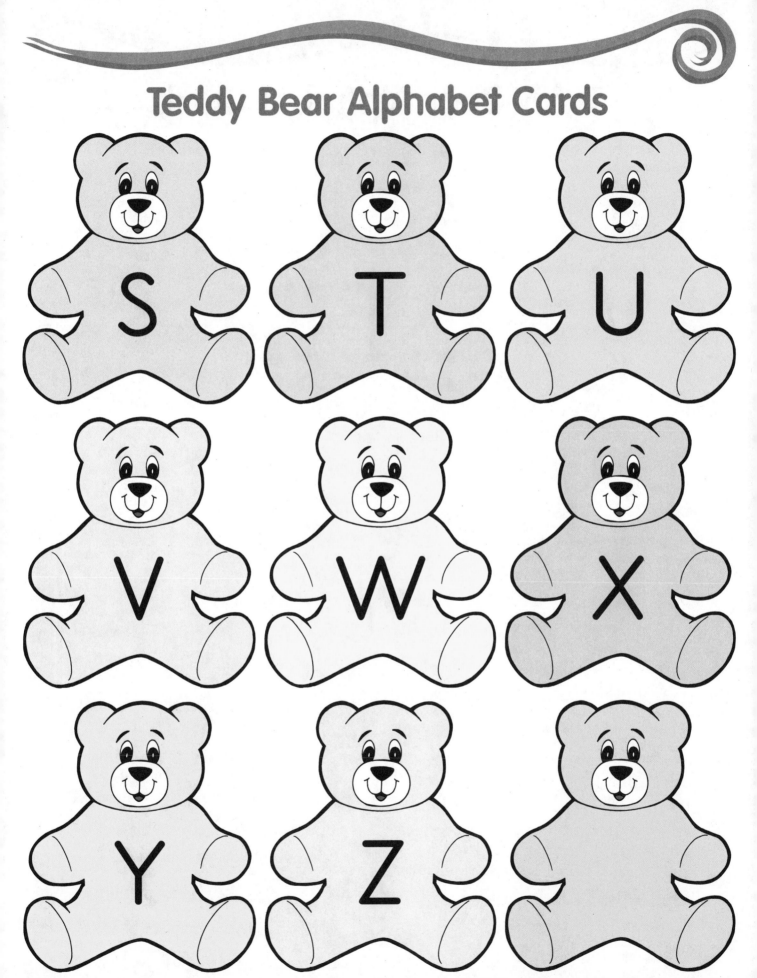

Teddy Bear Alphabet Cards

u   t   s

x   w   v

z   y

Draw the Room

Objective: Provides independent practice identifying letter sounds.

What You Will Need

- Draw the Room recording sheet (page 132)
- clipboards (optional) or stiff cardboard
- pencils or crayons

Create It

1. In the center provide pencils clipboards, and copies of the Draw the Room recording sheet for each student.

2. Program the recording sheets with the letter sounds being sought.

Teach It

Children will find things in the room that contain the sounds to be practiced. *Today we are going to draw some items in the room. We are going to look for things that contain the _____ sound.* On the class board, draw a chart that resembles the worksheet to be used with this activity.

Example: *Who can see something in the classroom that has a long /a/ sound in it?* A child raises his hand and answers: "table." *Good, now we will write the word "table' and draw a table next to it.* On the board, draw a picture of a table beside the /a/. Write the word with a long ā symbol on top of the "a." Then, on the line beside that, write the word "table." Follow this same process with the rest of the vowels.

Do this lesson with your students until you are confident they are able to do the center independently.

Teacher Tip

- Before a child does the activity, he or she needs to be able to distinguish different letter sounds.

Keep in Mind: The primary focus of this activity is to *hear* and i*dentify* sounds. Accept invented spelling.

Extension Idea

- Have students draw pictures of more than one item with the same sound.

Home Connection: Have students do this activity at home with items that can be found in their house. Program the recording sheets with the letter sounds before sending them home.

Draw the Room

Directions: Find something in the room that has the sound in the small box. Write the word and draw a picture of it in the larger box.

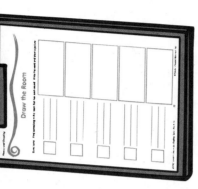

Draw the Room

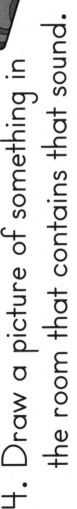

1. Put your paper on a clipboard.

2. Say the sound shown on your paper.

3. Write the word for that picture in the line provided.

4. Draw a picture of something in the room that contains that sound.

Sound Box Cards

Objective: Provides independent practice, decoding and spelling, through sound isolation.

What You Will Need

- Picture Cards (pages 139)
- small bowl or basket
- Sound Box Cards recording sheet (page 136)
- pencils

Create It

1. Place the picture cards in a container in the center.
2. Place the pencils and recording sheets near the container in the center.

Teach It

Today we are going to name all of the sounds we hear in a word. On the board draw the boxes to look like the boxes on the recording sheet. Choose a picture card out of the bowl or basket and show it to the students. *Of what is this a picture? Pig. What sound do you hear first? /p/* Write a **p** in the first box on the board. *What sound do you hear last? /g/* Write a **g** in the last box on the board. *Finally, what middle sound(s) do you hear? Write them in the middle box(es).* Do this lesson with your students until you are confident they are able to do the center independently.

Teacher Tips

- Choose three-letter or four-letter picture cards for the center.
- If you make additional cards, be careful to choose words, or pictures that do not have silent beginning or ending letters (knight, knee, hive).

Keep in Mind: Wait to fill in the middle sound boxes until the beginning and ending sounds have been filled in.

Extension Ideas

- Provide more difficult words as your students become more comfortable with their spelling. You may want to eventually use words that contain silent or "sleeping" letters and vowel combinations.
- Create more words for your students to write in the boxes provided by cutting out simple pictures from magazines.

Home Connection: Have students fill in sound boxes for things that can be found at home.

Sound Box Cards

Beginning	**Middle**	**Ending**

Beginning	**Middle**	**Ending**

Sound Box Cards

Beginning	**Middle**	**Middle**	**Ending**

Beginning	**Middle**	**Middle**	**Ending**

Sound Box Cards

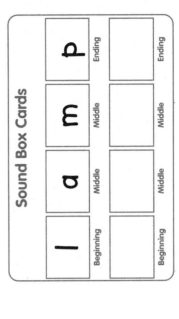

Sound Box Cards			
I	a	m	p
Beginning	Middle	Middle	Ending
Beginning	Middle	Middle	Ending

1. Choose a picture card and name the picture.

2. Write the beginning sound you hear in the first box.

3. Write the ending sound in the last box.

4. Write the middle sound you hear in the middle box or boxes.

5. Blend the sounds together and say the word again.

Scavenger Hunt for Sounds

Objective: Provides independent practice identifying letters and sounds.

What You Will Need
- Teddy Bear Alphabet Cards (pages 125–130)
- Scavenger Hunt for Sounds recording sheet (page 142)
- pencils, crayons, and markers

Create It
1. Use a set of Teddy Bear Alphabet Cards, or prepare another set by writing the alphabet on small pieces of square construction paper.
2. Copy the Scavenger Hunt for Sounds recording sheet.
3. Arrange the cards, the recording sheets, and the writing tools in the center.

Teach It

Today we are going on a sound hunt. We are going to look for things that have the sound shown on the card. Show the students the Teddy Bear Alphabet Card you have chosen. *What letter is this? What sound does this letter make? Let us look around the room for items that have this sound at the beginning of the word (or at the end of the word.)* Show students how to complete the Scavenger Hunt for Sounds recording sheet or do the activity on plain paper.

Do this lesson with your students until you are confident they are able to do the center independently.

Teacher Tip
- Make certain you have appropriate items to find in your classroom. It would be a good idea to "plant" items in your room if you are working on a specific sound.

Keep in Mind: Some beginning sounds are difficult to find in a classroom. Be open to creativity or delete some letters from the activity.

Extension Ideas
- Have students write words that begin or end with the first letter of their first or last name.

- Have student hunt for items in the classroom that *end* in the sound shown on the card.

Home Connection: Have students go on a Scavenger Hunt for Sounds at home or on a nature walk.

Scavenger Hunt for Sounds

Hunt for [   ] sounds.

Write the words you found that contain the _____ sound.

_____

- -

1. _____

_____

- -

2. _____

_____

- -

3. _____

Draw a picture to represent one of the words.

Scavenger Hunt for Sounds

-A-

1. Choose an alphabet letter card.

2. Say the letter name.

3. Say the sound the letter makes.

4. Write that letter on the recording sheet.

5. Find items that begin with the sound the letter makes.

6. Draw a picture of one of the words.

Reading and Writing Response Centers

5 W's and an H

The Letter Kid

Storyboards

Favorite Part Illustration

Dramatization

Book Report

Notes

_____

_____

_____

_____

_____

_____

_____

_____

_____

_____

_____

5 W's and an H

Objective: Provides independent practice with reading, with comprehension, and with critical thinking.

What You Will Need

- any text
- square gift box
- plain paper or contact paper
- tape
- scissors
- markers
- packing peanuts (or something comparable)
- 5 W's and an H recording sheet (page 148)
- Optional: labels (page 151)

Create It

1. Fill the box with packing peanuts.
2. Seal the box and wrap it with plain paper or contact paper.
3. On each side of the box write a question word: **Who, What, Where, When, Why,** and **How** or use the labels on page 151.

Teach It

Read a book together in class. When you have completed the story, ask the children questions using the words *Who, What, Where, When, Why,* and *How.* Show the students the Question Cube. Read another story together with the class. *Let's roll the Question Cube and answer questions about the story we just read.* Demonstrate rolling the cube and asking questions about it prompted by the word on the cube. When students are ready, group them in pairs and have them "partner read" a story. Then, they can use the cube to ask each other questions regarding the text. Explain to your students that they need to write the answers to the questions on the recording sheet. Do this lesson with your students until you are confident they are able to do the center independently.

Teacher Tip

- If students aren't able to read aloud to each other, use a story line you have read to the class.

Keep in Mind: Students may get off task during this activity. Remind students that they must take turns "asking" and "answering" the questions.

Extension Idea

- Use the cube to make up stories.

Home Connection: Have students write a question for each W and H word about a family member's job.

5 W's and an H

Directions: Answer each question as you roll the specific question word on the Question Cube.

Title:

_____

- -

_____

Who was the character?

_____

- -

_____

What did he or she do?

_____

- -

_____

Where did he or she do it?

_____

- -

_____

When did he or she do it?

_____

- -

_____

Why did he or she do it?

_____

- -

_____

How did he or she solve the problem?

_____

- -

_____

5 W's and an H

1. Read a story.

2. Take turns rolling the cube.

3. Read the question word on the cube.

4. Answer the question and write down the response.

5. Keep rolling the Question Cube until all the questions are answered.

5 W's and an H

Glue or tape these question words to your cube.

Who?

What?

When?

Where?

Why?

How?

The Letter Kid

Objective: Provides independent practice composing a letter and incorporating the different parts of a letter.

What You Will Need

- The Letter Kid (boy) and The Letter Kid (girl) recording sheets (pages 157–158)
- Blank Letter Form (page 154)
- pencils
- The Letter Kid poster (page 157)

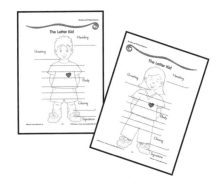

Create It

1. Make copies of the Letter Kids and the Blank Letter Form.
2. Provide the above-mentioned items in a center.
3. Post the Letter Kid poster in the center.

Teach It

Students will compose a letter. Make a copy of The Letter Boy or The Letter Girl on a transparency. Using the overhead, demonstrate proper letter writing technique and review letter components, including the heading, greeting, body, closing, and signature. *This guide will help us remember the parts of a letter. Let's look at the picture and decide how it will help us remember each part of a letter. The heading is when we write the date at the top of the letter. Think of your head being on top of your body; the heading is at the top of the letter. When we greet someone in person, we speak to the person using our mouth. Our mouth is at the top of our body, and the greeting is at the top of the letter.* Fill in the greeting part of a letter. *Many important parts of our body are in the middle, or our torso. The main part of a letter is in the middle.* Fill in the body part of the letter. *When we leave from somewhere, we use our feet to move. Our feet are at the bottom of our body. We close a letter when we want to say goodbye. The closing of a letter is at the bottom of a letter.* Close the letter. *Lastly, we sign our name at the bottom of the letter to say who the letter is from.* Do this lesson with your students until you are confident they are able to do the center independently.

Teacher Tip

- Review the Letter Kid poster often. Have students stand up and point to their own bodies and state what part of a letter each part represents.

Keep in Mind: Give your students lots of opportunities to write letters.

Extension Ideas

- Write a get-well note.
- Write a thank-you note.

Home Connection: Have students write a letter to a family member who does not live at their house.

Blank Letter Form

_____

_____

_____

_____ ,

_____

_____

_____

_____

_____

_____ ,

_____

_____

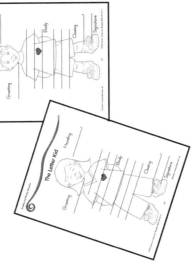

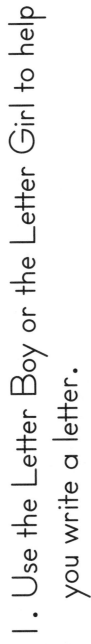

The Letter Kid

1. Use the Letter Boy or the Letter Girl to help you write a letter.

2. Write a letter to a friend.

3. Check your writing for all of the letter parts.

Heading: Your eyes look at a calendar to find the date.

Greeting: Say hello to the person to whom you are writing.

Body: The body is the heart of the letter.

Closing: The closing ties it all together. (Say goodbye.)

Signature: Who wrote the letter?

The Letter Kid

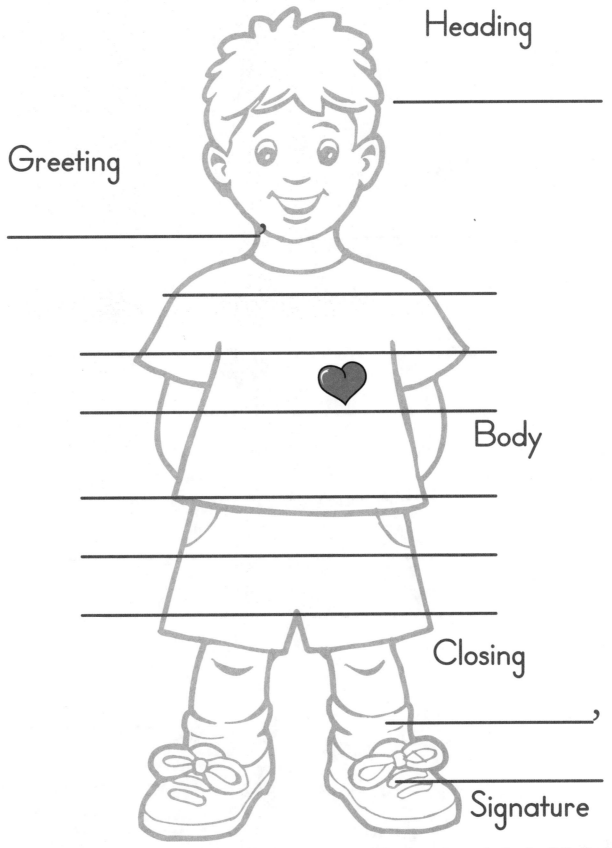

Heading

_____

Greeting

_____

_____

_____

_____

Body

_____

_____

_____

Closing

_____ ,

_____

Signature

The Letter Kid

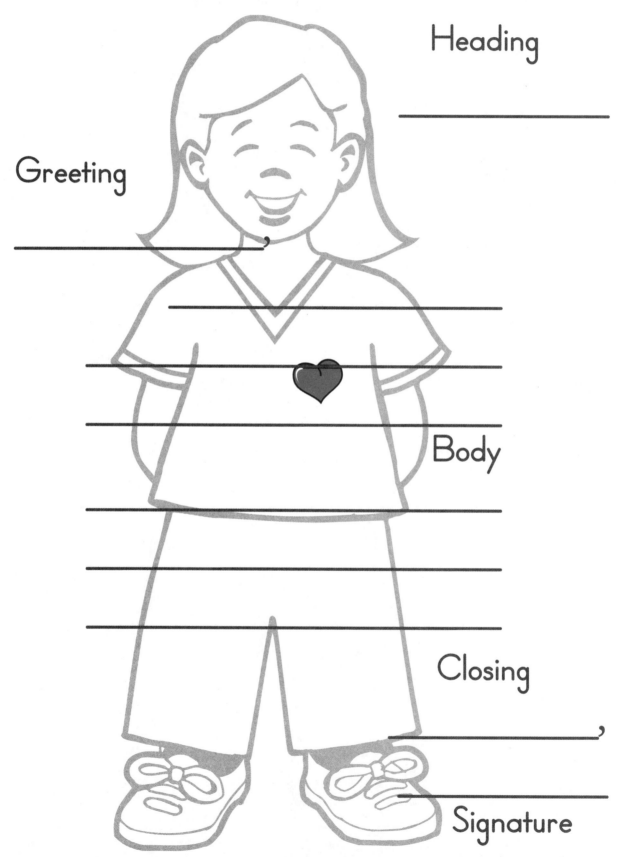

Heading

Greeting

Body

Closing

,

Signature

Storyboards

Objective: Provides independent practice in writing, comprehension, and story order.

What You Will Need

- any text
- Storyboards recording sheet (page 160)
- writing and drawing tools

Create It

1. Make copies of the Storyboards recording sheet.
2. Provide the items listed above at a center.

Teach It

Today we are going to make a storyboard for a story we have read. A "storyboard" is something that tells a summary of a story. The storyboard allows us to tell what happened in the beginning, the middle, and the end of a story. Read a story with the class. Draw four boxes on the board, chart, butcher paper, or an overhead. *Who can tell me what happened at the beginning of the story.* After ideas have been shared, have a student draw a picture that summarizes the beginning in the first box. Next, do the same activity regarding the middle of the story and have a student draw a picture in the second box. *Who would like to draw what happened in the middle of the story?* Complete the activity with the picture of the end of the story in the third box. *Who would like to draw the ending to the story?*

Do this lesson with your students until you are confident they are able to do the center independently.

Teacher Tip

- This activity works best with fictional or narrative stories instead of fact-based resource text.

Keep in Mind: Drawing the story parts takes a lot more time than telling what happened.

Extension Ideas

- Make a Storyboards recording sheet with 3 spaces for younger storytellers.
- Encourage your students to write a brief synopsis of each part of the letter.

Home Connection: Have students tell their own story in storyboard form.

Storyboards

Storyboards

1. Read the story.

2. Draw a picture that tells about *the beginning* in the first box.

3. Draw pictures that tells about *the middle* in the second and third boxes.

4. Draw a picture that tells about *the end* in the last box.

5. Write about each picture.

Storyboards

First Spot went outside.

Then I went out to play with Spot.

Next _____

Finally We went to sleep.

Favorite Part Illustration

Objective: Provides independent practice reading, comprehending, and story retelling through drawing.

What You Will Need

- an assortment of books
- drawing paper
- colored pencils, markers, crayons, etc.
- optional: Favorite Part Illustration recording sheet.

Create It

1. Provide the items noted above in a center.
2. If possible, add fun pens to the collection.

Teach It

Read some stories with your students. Ask students to describe their favorite parts. *Today, we are going to read some stories and talk about our favorite parts. As you listen, think about what you like best. Is it the characters, the setting, the action, or something else? Draw a picture of your favorite part.*

Do this lesson with your students until you are confident that they are able to do the center procedures independently.

Teacher Tip

- Children tend to "copy" one another's ideas. Remind students that their favorite part is probably different from their friend's favorite part. Encourage children to select different stories/parts to talk about. If someone mentions a child's favorite part, let him or her acknowledge the fact and then choose a "second" favorite part.

Extension Ideas

- Write a sentence describing your favorite part of a story.
- Act out your favorite part of a story.

Home Connection: Have students draw a picture of their favorite book at home. Write a few sentences explaining why it is their favorite book.

Favorite Part Illustration

Name: ....

Title: ....

Directions: Draw a picture of your favorite part of the book.

Favorite Part Illustration

1. Read a story.

2. Draw a picture of your favorite part.

Dramatization

Objective: Provides independent practice in reading and comprehension, as well as public speaking and drama.

What You Will Need

- any story
- props (optional)
- costumes (optional)
- Dramatization recording sheet (page 168)
- writing tools

Create It

1. After the children have read a story, provide an area for reenacting the story.
2. Provide props and costumes to enhance the dramatization.

Teach It

"Dramatization" is a big word that means retelling a story. When we want to retell a story we need to think about the characters, the props, and the clothes (costumes) the characters wore. As a class, demonstrate reenacting stories by coaching students through various parts. Remind students about dialogue and mannerisms. Stress the importance of sticking to the story through the important elements.

Do this lesson with your students until you are confident they are able to do the center independently.

Teacher Tips

- Children will need a lot of room for this activity.
- Give the actors time to "rehearse" and then provide students with a full class audience for their presentations. Let your students practice describing their characters.

Keep in Mind: Speaking in front of others is very natural for some and very difficult for others. Remind students to give participants equal time.

Extension Ideas

- Have your students write about and draw a picture of the character they are playing on the Dramatization recording sheet.
- Put on a class play. Invite parents to come watch the performance.

Home Connection: Have the students put on a play at home of their favorite story. Have family members play some of the roles.

Dramatization

Directions: Write a description of your character.

Directions: Draw a picture of your character.

Dramatization

1. Read a story.

2. Decide how to retell the story.

3. Get props and costumes.

4. Act out the story.

5. Write a description and draw a picture of your character.

Book Report

Objective: Provides independent practice reading, writing, and reasoning.

What You Will Need

- Book Report recording sheets (pages 172, 175, 176)
- pencils, crayons, and/or markers
- transparencies (optional)

Create It

1. Make copies of the appropriate Book Report recording sheets or provide drawing paper.
2. Provide the items noted above at a center.

Teach It

Read a book with your students. Copy one of the Book Report recording sheets onto a transparency and share it with the students. *Today we are going to work on a book report. A "book report" is a summary of a book you have read. We will share information about what we have read. Our information will give other people an idea of what the book was about.* Work with the students to complete the book report recording sheets. Allow time for illustrations.

Do this lesson with your students until you are confident they are able to do the center independently.

Teacher Tip

- Some students may be more comfortable drawing a picture. Later, help them label their drawings.

Keep in Mind: Before doing the Book Report recording sheets independently, it may help your students to discuss their favorite parts as a class.

Extension Idea

- Have students share their book with the class using a Book Report recording sheet as a guide. Share the illustration as well.

Home Connection: Have each student ask a family member about one of his or her favorite books. Then, the student can complete a Book Report recording sheet based on the information the family member provided.

Book Report

My name
_____
- -
_____

Name of the book
_____
- -
_____

Author
_____
- -
_____

Book Report

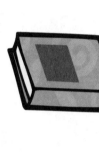

1. Read a book.

2. Do one of the Book Report recording sheets.

3. Draw a picture about the book.

4. Share your work with the class.

Book Report

Title: _____

Circle the correct sentence. Color the matching face.

I liked this book very much.   ☺

I liked this book a little.   😐

I did not like this book.   ☹

Reason: _____

_____

_____

_____

_____

_____

Book Report

Name:

_____

- -

_____

Title:

_____

- -

_____

Author:

_____

- -

_____

Summary:

_____

- -

_____

_____

- -

_____

_____

- -

_____

- -

_____